THE HOUSE THAT MANDA BUILT

NICKI JACKOWSKA

The House
That Manda Built

LONDON
THE MENARD PRESS
1981

THE HOUSE THAT MANDA BUILT

© Nicki Jackowska 1980
ISBN 0 903400 60 X

Frontispiece drawing by Andrzej Jackowski

The Menard Press acknowledges financial support
from the Arts Council of Great Britain

The Menard Press is a member of ALP

Menard Press books are distributed in North America by
SPD Inc. 1636 Ocean View Avenue, Kensington, California 94707

The Menard Press
8 The Oaks, Woodside Avenue,
London N12 8AR

Printed by Skelton's Press Limited
Wellingborough, Northamptonshire, England

ACKNOWLEDGEMENTS
Some of these poems have appeared in the following
publications:
Adad; Ambit; Chicago Tribune Magazine; Contemporary
Women Poets (Rondo); Deep Earth Review; Gallery;
Janus (USA); Last Fly; Little Word Machine; New Poetry;
Omens; Phantom Captain Book of Forewords; Poetry of the
Seventies (Rondo); Poetry Review; Poetry St Ives;
Poetry South-East 1 (S.E. Arts); Poetry South-East 4 (S.E. Arts);
Prospice; Resurgence; Samphire; Sceptre Press; Second Aeon;
Tangent; Words Press; X-Press.

'My Master Comes and Goes' and 'The King Rises' were
published as a booklet *The King Rises* by Second Aeon
Publications.
'Nightride' forms part of a longer poem, published as a
booklet *Nightride* by Aquila.
'Between the She-Devil and the Deep Blue Earth' is part of
the poem-sequence *The Words That Manda Spoke*, published
by Bridgewest Publications. It was also runner-up in the
Transatlantic Review Erotica Competition.
'The House That Manda Built' and 'House of Twelve Names'
have been published as *The Bone Palaces* by Omens Press.
'Queen of Clay' and 'The Girl Within the Wheel' have been set to
music by Ian Lamb and were first performed by The Wyvern
Ensemble at the Guildhall, Leicester, September 1980.
'My Master Comes and Goes' and 'A Month of Small Guests'
have been broadcast on BBC Radio 3 Poetry Now.

The author wishes to express her thanks to the Society of
Authors for a grant during the writing of this collection.

MANDA AND THE STONES

Manda threw stones into the garden pond,
one for an eye, two for a tooth
he sung, and the stones fell plop into the pool.

He would build a city of stones
and they eyed him from the rock-beds.
He sung, and each stone departed from its earth.

I'll need a locksmith for the gates, he said,
grazing their skins. One face digging deep
into its parent stone, turned ghost

and marked the days. Forty days
he swung through, lifting and parting.
The building grew like a Babel tower

and its voices, one for a day, chimed
the seasons' turning, histories of all
the gathering earths. Until Manda's dream

of Albion hung like a coat of many stones
over his strawberry beds and runner-beans,
for the garden bore its house like a mascot.

All the lucky stones, each chosen rock
hung together with a noise of fallen buildings.
Manda's face grinned through the jaws of the ruined city.

1 August 1980

For Andrzej and Laura
Also for my Mother and Father

CONTENTS

MY MASTER COMES AND GOES

1
The master is here. He quite overcomes me.
He cries like a baby in the first shallows
And must be stroked awake
Out of his mad head. His bed is nettles
That kiss and silk his nightwalks
Through passages that run with stings.
He is a giant beetle with luminous green back
I can ride to sweetmeats and ripe gardens.

2
Later he grows. He changes colour even.
His coat is pitted with ends of rainbows,
They drive spears from their colour-tournaments
Through his space, and colours run
On his wet landscapes washed ambers and cerise.
Sometimes he curls and draws in his parts
And comes back hard and perfect like a marble bullet
Straight to the heart. The caught milkwhorl
Explodes, and it rains through the cavities
With milk like blossom.
In this hard round ball, he crashes through
Flesh like a painted bull.

3
He is a flower in an eggshell that waits its time.
The faces are hatched over mine,
They wobble and tease
And I can no longer be sure of the mirror.
When there is no other sound
He presses against my eardrums and whispers his charm,
His feet dance down my ears
Their patter is the distant click of a cricket.

4
He leaves in the last flutter of a drowned moth,
In the coiled spring of life, spiralling out.

5
My master uncurls ribbons out of your mouth,
He unravels slowly.
Your tongue is a pink lizard
Which is his finger.
The noise it points is the music of stones
And the notes settle and form,
They are gleaming monuments in wordbeds of stones.

6
He is the barbed elf, the branded head,
The single eye in a ruby chalice,
The peachcore, the thorn that laughs as it bites.
The locked box of dreams, with twin mice to guard it,
The split moon, the green edge of a flameface.
He is the hippopotamus with a snake's head,
The frog with a violin in its mouth,
The right piece of the cake,
The ripped buglenote of petrified town band.
He is the tree that yawns its trunk and bellows leaves,
The rose that will not bloom quiet.
He is a fruit of fur,
He is the happy creak of the splintered cross,
The right-handed lily,
The budding limb that the head grows
To find new places.
He is tumbled head and crumbling stone,
The witches joke, the trick of wizards,
The mirror, the splinter, the shriek, the cat,
He is the broken pattern in an old carpet of dust.

SONG FOR THE BEGINNING OF IT

The morning is in
takes the sky on its tongue;
trickle of light down the sides of hills,
and it is a huge flower, streaming.

The noise of it bellows in the black hollows
and they unfold themselves;
thousands of bellflowers nod to it,
priest of the hills bows to it;

where it began, a hidden pulse
of rose. the waters shiver
the shock of it upon them, silver,
woke the house, the window

is in flames. I see
a torch. It fans the fire nearer.

I am alight
and the fire swallows me.

THE DRESSING ROOM

It is a sound like roses bursting, an infinite cradle
of sound as each petal thunders to its close.
She enters from behind the mirror wearing opal and
spilling words that were white photographs. He
can only see his own face, tooth, word, nail,
excrement, a dusty bouquet laid at her feet.
She enters from behind the mirror wearing bones.

She treads him carefully under the glass case,
particularly. She watches his mouth make all the
shapes of its invention. He is wearing noisy
cloth like a mandrake. Abduction forms behind the
roses, witch-formation of crow-greetings. A long
red nail blisters his glass prison.
It is a sound like petals applauding.

I welcome you, Mr. Dionys,
says the mistress of a rapacious supper waiting
on the table. Apples longing for their enzymes,
eager to be split.
His heart beats mercilessly where she first felled
him. The mirrors feel unclean. In them he sees
hands reaching for love in all the world-cathedrals
and hill-palaces. Hands with an ache and an itch
and the wind blowing through them. His own hands,
lizards on the bare earth, scaley instruments
creeping across her flesh, etching his name.

She wondered if she could include him in the
amphitheatre of her heart.

My tongue has a knot which I can't unravel, he
says. And drinks to it. I am waiting for a
gilt-edged night and the clock mean as a knife.
I have been too long in this place and my chair
will not let me go. The fruit is full of malice
and skins that remind me of my heart.

14

She came from behind the mirror and her mouth wore
red and spoke like a hot geranium.
He ate of it greedily.
Laid out on the table, she was his perfect host,
willing to please, bared to receive him, powdered
into a white replica, and her death did not make
him bleed, as he had hoped it would.

SOLSTICE

Candles bursting
out of my head
The loose wolf of sorrow
snuffling under my skirts

Bending under illegal air
A banishment

Moving among grasses
wearing badges of failure
I come to the crepuscule
mad country of the moth

BETWEEN THE SHE-DEVIL
AND THE DEEP BLUE EARTH
(From: The Words That Manda Spoke)

There is something buzzing in the clothes.
she breathes me out through the long thin reed of her
nightie. turn over, she says, and I roll like a
plum in her mouth.
the ghost in his windingsheet has left a plate of
stars to bite. their eyes glint out of the black
box, the book of dreams, the furry velvet under the
bed. they are sucked out of the black like fruits
for picking. they are white fists in the night
clothes.

the bed is long and lined with woods.
a pink harp that beats its strings against the sheets.
a thicket to walk in where the twigs are short and curly.
avenues alive with shadows.
the long corridors lined with colours that talk,
green telling of lace, the pink of maps,
the blue of an icicle she melted yesterday.
turn back, she says, and I roll like a bead down her sides.

She is too hot for the laundered morning, the table
of dew, the damp meeting across white plains. the
grapefruit hisses in her hot mouth.
the piano skids white teeth across flesh of silk, biting
the skin, shredding the crusts, a staircase of dominoes,
the black and white fruits of her. my table stretches
from her to when the next one comes. I bite at the
sound which is crimson and set like her mouth. the
years' grasses slip in between. the years' forests
gallop across our eyes. the drops fall from stars to
neck with face sliced in between like cool lemons. I
can taste ripe grass, the green sound of lawns.
trickling sound of flowers streaking open, the waking
flower is a spiral of beads. we count the way to
the centre, a clicking march of yellow pollen.
Her bath is of the waters of the green lawn.

I am still marching up and down stairs, demanding the
fruits she laid in the night, cold without my protective
woollens. my long scarf is still wound round the
bedpost and strangles the woodenface of the peeping
tom who watches over us.
rub my back, she says, and I drop stitches running
upstairs through the soap, shedding five more skins,
shivering near to the bone. when the taps sink
malignant teeth into my wet hollows, I am water-logged.
but I must splash to her, peeling off my scales, which
adhere to all the large fleshy areas like small tissue
maps, heavy with patterns, forgetting my boots which
make inky prints all over her back. we swim off for
supplies in the light of a hungry lightbulb.
pass the soap, she says, and I skid all down a lavender
bank, where her skin hollows into purple flowers. and
I must bite them like she tells me, with my tongue first
to sound out the land, and then take the flower between
the teeth, gently, like bursting the ripe skins of
plums. I can't read the letters that go skidding
away, curled up like water-lilies in sleep. there
are other things too that dance and twist in the
current, all tunnelling down the pipes, their backs
turned, little black charts and guides that smile as
they vanish. I am a large fish left behind, and can't
get my nose down the grid. there is the sound of damp
leaves and the sea waving fronds of water in the jet
where they go. and then I must start on the knees.

The bed sings like a linnet. or the inside of a ripe
fruit. the covers flap like dark birds of prey.
they hang still over where I have landed, waiting for
the dark to work. she trails her dress like old
newspapers, yellowing.

but all her skins hum like a chorus of young girls
in a large cathedral, where the few candles make
the sound a gilded spiral to the dark arches. I

can follow her through to the bending songs, and the
whole dark edifice comes nearer. I can trail my
fingers over the smooth stones, and they soften
in the teeth like the fruits she promised me, which
didn't come yesterday.

I eat purple cloths and am a castle of quiet shadows.
sun turns in under the hedges.
my fur is frosty.
nuts are split open by dark teeth, by winter ivories.
nuts are split and it is a new shoot of steel,
and the snail's eye.
I am so many skins away from him, she said.

LETTER TO THE PRIEST OF THE GARDEN

My mirror is empty like a winter earth
no face shines there, no ghost moving
my mirror talks like an old giant
of monumental candles, of great
boulders, the breaking of furnaces

life waits on the other side, bright
as a bead or a shed tear
it waits like a crystal, a glass knot
it waits quietly like a nun
to be unravelled. I move towards it
carefully cutting the thorns

the ink is shed from today's wound
the ink runs like sap from my dry fingers
I am waiting in my pearly jar
I am writing names with my frost-breath
the flowers bend under the weight
of winter candles

THE HOUSE THAT MANDA BUILT

The garden. the man sits on his woodenstep and commands
his acres. his own small garden is landscaped in stone.
he creeps like an alleycat over the edges of his vegetable
patch, a heap of old bones. decaying bricks mangled taps
and drains. dark corridors between the leaves. his city
patch. his carefully matured stone ingredients.
he has watched her come out of his garden and copies her
for his album. pressed between pages locked in a box at
the back of a cupboard the key on a string lowered out of
the attic window. pale paper woman he takes out and
smoothes. soon he will lie with her between the books.
ironed out of light. a dark tissue. pressed in a thin
ecstasy against paper thighs.

The grass climbs higher. in the green grass-cloth he
weaves his table and chair, and sits in the green shade
thinking green thoughts of her.
Yesterday he was generous with his large leaden weights.
scattered them wild over the garden, backs of chairs,
rafters. his soup tasted of molten copper. the bread
bit his teeth. he spits that out. the crumbs rattle
on the stones like bullets. he left it all to harden
in the sun.
And the roses. they wore his weights like medallions.
drooping heads, and the whole flower-bed a clanking
chorus in his iron masque. until even she freezes in
his metal groin.
There is a huge pack of yapping stones, pebbles with a
thin high squeak and the great deep bark of a boulder. they
are the priests, their black rags flutter like torn birds.
His army marches steadfastly before him. first come the
grasses, jackbooted roots. last in the line she fires a
shot. it scorches the garden and blows steam in his face.
the dying roots give off the odour of damp socks, and his
face grows thin in the sun.

Carving her mouth in the tree's trunk, spends long hours
glued to the bark. bites off her lips and swallows them.
patches up the wound with moss to muffle the noise.
he plucks out the eye from a daisy, insisting it had been
watching him for days.

They are liars the four earths.
The line of them shivers. the heat of them watches her
dresses unwrap. the dark of them paints her indigo.
their fire eats her fingers and feet like a slow feast.
out of his mouth, out of his dark, she runs silky. he
is exploded in many days of dancing. and she is behind
the dark where his breath thickens.
the mind of a plant is his picture book. her open pages.
tissue petals read in to the centre.
her magic entrances. her budding scarves to bind his
eyes.

Today he will make another room for his house. the last
year's polygonum seeds in the nursery and a forest cradles
the small things that there almost breathe. he can peer
down the green to the rocking crib and the bear that
whispers. her dolls stare. the bricks build one tier
and then fall down. his fingers push among the quilts
and covers for the heart of her, but here are icy sheets.
he makes a small shape for the bed but the stuffing bleeds.
soon he will make a darker room, a black room with fringes
and laces and satins. the window painted out and a carpet
of fur. his fingers are busy with wood and nails. perhaps
she will like it better. his house is in bud.

Between the she-devil and the deep blue earth is the rod
of glass. it is a lever to open gates.
between the she-devil and the deep blue earth is a house
of glass, with glass door-knockers and glass curtains to
shut out the light that rains its dust on all the glass
mirrorbeds.
the rod of glass looks with its one eye. it stands
firm between he and she like a dictionary. they feed

it with a little oil and old libraries.
he has lost the polishing cloth. some of the windows
have stars and are growing grasses on their sills. some
of the beds wear covers like silly dresses. the fireplace
is disguised as a letter-box and all the letters burn.

Where she fell, a flower grows. it is small and tired
and has a tissue of dust on the petals. he passed it
by, taking it for a bead that fell from her throat. a
drop in the fountain of words she spoke to open the door.
and enter invisible.

Between the she-devil and the glass-house, hot plants in
the alcoves. her order of marching pinned up over the
bookcases.
she inserts a finger carefully into the slot and the whole
wall shivers and tinkles like a glass tree in heat. she
conjures children who run in and out of the wall wet from
its rain. it is their glass fountain.
and it is time to go to birth. a dark curtain folded over
her face. a lace handkerchief. the creamy morning etched
on the opposite wall. and she, seen through to the bone.

She softly rides in and out of his head on her young grey
feet with little pinches and a few words dropped into the
bag where he collects ancient sayings and pulls them out
in tired times like strips of magic tape. and binds his eyes.
Where she enters, a pink shell. he hears her come a
spiralling horse. the weeds overlap and make a singing
canopy where they rub together. the trees are molten.
And the snake has bitten. she looks for the spot to suck
the poison. her child kissed by the snake and must run
as the bite runs. and the body full with the dark.
earth listens, buckles and curls. arches and makes white lace
over its head. a bridal morning. she is forced open by the
soft gold candle. the flame that has burned out her eyes and
made two dark pits to swim in.
The woollen canopy. where she weaves her new eyes out of
spun plants. the lens of the rose. the eyeglass where

a tree sits blinking. he makes the morning a large lazy
eye. opening and shutting the house where they all sleep
in a glass bowl. an itching of many small threads of light
that bind the bed into a flame.
Her name was not known. she lived between two words, a
perpetual haitus. open doors, and his red tongue licking
up the weeds. his other hand strokes the hair that grows
in the porch. her unknown pulse.
the best he could do was to stitch her up roughly round the
edges, using an old thread he had once followed to her centre.
where he tied the knot was a scar she said was a birthmark.
it bled coloured juices and she saw the world through its reds.
until she thought it had always been there and the house was
pink and tasted of strawberries.
Out of the top drawer, a left leg. he sorted through her
clothes, looking for the final garment. all he could find
was yesterday's skin.
the night opens its gills. the iron grins. her dark
skirts have an itchy glitter, and where she tries to pick
the stars they bleed white rain. it pours through the
holes like kisses and they are pins in the heart. like the
flying spittle of gnats.
she wears her words like a showgirl. her rosette wishes
wind snakes in and out of her legs. where he bit her, a
black bush in flames.
He opens the book and she rises from her sleep like an old
story, her pages torn. a grated fish bone. a pack of
blue cotton reels. a weedy plain with yellow spots. her
attributes are enormous. she buttons up the rose at her
throat and grows into a starbud that will one day be a black sun.

The eyelet of glass. the word seen through. the paper
of winds that tear his handmaidens. time cutting out
his name and it waters the sky. it waters the words. it
waters his house of bones.
caught in his foot, a frog in laughter. rusty ointments
for the floor's big wound. and he told her she smelt
sweet and of muskroses but she wouldn't show her roomsecret.
The incision. the scissornoise. her legs rapping at

the edge of the pain like pins in his last year's head.
the ivory he grew yesterday. a statue of wet silk scrapes
its way on to him with slippers of silky steel.
the inn of the bed.
the block of light that goes tumbling down his head like
old luminous staircases,
and he made her a canopy of spiderdreams. she sleeps
beneath their black lace.
The reason for starfall a patch of burnt anemones. crusts
of old dead poppies. a half-eaten rose.
the priest of the bed wears woollen mittens. the chilly
sheets have hurt his hands.
his right hand is a barbed sword. the left a limpet.
the crack in the bed is his parrying-place, his old
gemstone watch. it ticks him in and out of crevices
like a hunted beetle.

Thats my blood making the rose red, he said, picking the
thorns from his hands.
he creeps warily into sunday. scraping of chalk in the
aisle. buzzing in the font. communion of legs.
his thought makes him walk on cushions, and spray the
priest with dust.

Nighttime and the dread of walls. his heart in a bag
starched stiff for safety. his legs in steel tubes in
case they drop off. the geraniums lined up in rows to
be counted. his head under the pillow for fear of being
seen. the rotting of many plants under his window keeping
him awake at night. his dreams are brown and smell of
dead flowers. he wraps his head around a stone, and it
gives off words like fine chippings.

His house ticks.
deep in its heart is a stirring of worm. a thrashing
of mandibles. wind hooks through the knots and looks
for new names to bite. he sees pink tissue roll inwards
to centre of flower he planted under it. he sees large
pink flower undulate like underwater mouth. he sees

moon crushed in his fist like pale handkerchief. he sees
rocks crease like tinfoil and open wounds in rockpools.
his edifice is cracking.
he watered it yesterday. but the skin is scaley and
sucked up all the moisture through its crust. he plunges
into lizard mouth to pick the flower and the petals
sizzle. they are hot coals that sheath him. they
blacken his edifice and he curls into one of its mouths
and beseeches it. creeps up its back passage and beats
on the walls. wind hatches out ancient hammers of sound
that scrape and whine among his bones. light hisses
down and snakes his limbs with heavy metal.
people thicken. they have lived there too long. they
are crusted and blacken the sun he made. accumulate
around the heart and clog the arteries. he is a thin
beam of irridescent bone up to his neck in fingers.
and he can see that his edifice is splintering. it
is dry with the licking of tongues. it needs oil and
the glint of a mirror. new winters. iceclean.

He watches the house shrink into his head and stands alone
among the boulders. out of the stones the cry of a
snake. out of the snake a blue wind. out of the wind
a sound of wood. and the wood marked with signs. and
the signs the patterns for tomorrow's stones.

AUGUST THIEF

She strips the house of its peeling paint and
it is white and boney like a man with no
fruits.
She strips the washing-line of shirts and
there are only phantoms chattering in the
wind.
Looking for cores, she peels apples until
they are bled.
Coloured confections fly from her cupboards
like wild confetti after the hunt. Her
heart hammers like an iron nightingale.

She peers under the skin of a water-bubble
let loose from the mirror, looking for
captured storms.
She hunts another season's flower, folded
upon itself.
Until the house is twisted like a huge
spiral screw and the plants are etched into
graffiti on the stone wall, and the washing
is forged into metal arabesques and the
white lid of summer is closed shut over
her head.

CONCERNING TRANSMISSIONS
AND AUNT ALICE

From: Dr Marbles and Marianne

Dear Godfrey,

I feel compelled to write to you and describe my
totally unexpected condition. I knew that I had
left the balcony-experiment behind, but am constantly
attacked by swarms of white dandelion hairs
that remind me of brides.
And breakfast is heavy with electrical messages that
sing among the cereal and interrupt my poached eggs
by infesting the knife and fork with spasms of
metallic trembling.
The words she lets fly are caught in a fine invisible
web of static that hangs like a cloud of bluebottles
over the marmalade.
I wish these friends – and their director, I suppose
it must be her – would be more considerate and
allow digestion. The table is an inferno of
cross-purposes. Nothing is clear Godfrey – I can't
find an exact quantification of meaning. I call for
an election, or a truce, but these invisible orators
obviously grow fat on the bursts of rage that
emanate at intervals from deep in my throat, like
puffs of encapsulated flame, mushroms of crimson
energy.
It doesn't matter where I am – in the house, or out
walking in the fields. When the mood takes them,
I am outwitted by seeds. I am laid bare by a
mere shiver on the air, the humming of invisible
riders – small ships of gleaming discoveries,
blueprints wrapped up in tiny crystal impulses
that inject me with what I can only think of as a
liquid so swift, it speeds to my heart before I
can capture it.
And what's worse, I cannot do my work. I spell
out the words of the telephone directory to

counteract these spells of weightlessness. I've
installed radios in my house, turned on night and
day. But the many silver buttons are alive with
dust and I can only hear other messages – of fire,
and the slow blue birth of an alien moon.
I scuttle like an itinerant crab beneath the
leather–bound voice that is the unacted sex
of my ageing aunt Alice. Her skirts seem to asbsorb
some of this mercury, this powder that knows each
gaping aperture, each entrance, each lobby, each cavity,
deserted for centuries. But then Aunt Alice is a
large area of inert bones, linked by a wasteland of
veins and arteries, hung with flesh stiff as a starched
tablecloth for the new monarch, embroidered with
initials of someone she has forgotten who never got
further than the border.
Yes, she knows how to manage Marianne and her
emanations. To enter Aunt Alice's house is to
receive the blessing of a cold dank hand, and hear
the laughter recede and the tickling words trail
down her flagged path like snails in flight. But I
cannot visit Aunt Alice without a tremble in the
bones, and the re-echo of gates slotting shut, of a
fading sun, and my heart pinned to a plate of bread
and butter and thin jam.
So, dear friend, I wage a war here in this thin few
feet of dancing cellular disorder. This is my last cry
for help, while even now the page opens under the
scalpel, splitting into a wound of slow rusty granite,
of a green luminous lady who wears thighs like
windows – and I, struggling to master a structure
so that I may transmit to you my distress, am even
now seeking that warm green moss which is called her
centre, and finding the greatest difficulty
constructing this frail bridge of straws to try and
reach you, over her opalescent flesh.
Please send me the following – (the noise is rising
to a thin silver scream, like a needle sewing
distant parts of me together. I must stop it before

the threads bind me completely, before I am become
a knot, apex of all unheard-of messages) – I need
a hammer, thick blanket – (I can hear stars whisper
inside the bedside clock), a wig of short dark hair –
could you manage a set of tubular bells? – I am running
out of batteries – a recipe for indigestion, herbs
various, tuning fork (perhaps if I unearth the piano . . . ?)
a beehive (with instructions), a new deck of cards,
a rope-ladder. But best of all Godfrey, if you could
manage a visit? My laboratory has taken a new
direction, and you were always a perfect gentleman
among vampires. . . .

Your affectionate Friend,

Marbles

THE FLOWER-WAKER

She is gone, and the sounds pour in.
the silence is drawing characters on
my distant skin. between them lie
unfinished faces, a garden with
histories flapping.
windows burn on the inside of stones.
I approach gratefully this place
where all lines meet.
my heart is an arena to find the
champion.

Monday

Monday is a crippled dog that reminds me of queens.
Monday is a garden roasted into hot air. A crow
refusing to take the veil. A man with a bird's
head staring at his reflection in my eye. Faces
falling slow as the sun from my book.

Tuesday

Tuesday grins like a lemon. Will squeeze the last
drop from a dry page. Wears a veil of mesh like a
collaborator. Issues a challenge among the falling
money and neat, corseted hours.
All the names are being written, are being burned.
Tight names, that will make the General, that will
lace him and button him, spur him and leather him,
shine in his boots and scream in the victory parade.
Black names of the priesthood written in charcoal
and sealingwax. Dark shadows chanting in the sacristy,
murmuring behind the font, pressed under his knees,
shivering among forbidden dreams folded among his
cloth.
Names of the woman who refuses to be photographed,
who will not speak one word for fear of stones.
Whose names crawl from the page, dissolve inside
the eyes of all her biographers and waits for the
second day to be bi-lingual.

Wednesday

She circles overhead looking for somewhere to plant
her new wife that is coming. She is a little larger
than her bed and has more entrances. She needs
ointments and oils for the skin that is expanding.
Grease for new hinges. Wax for the passageways. She
needs a large quiet garden for the new head to breathe,
and an extra room, for visitors, (who are also a little
larger than before).

Thursday

Crosses and flowers. Stars and fractures.
So far the joints are holding.
She grafts an erodite horizon on to the renograde
woman under a molecular sky. It is raining mercurial
shapes that might tie her to earth. These streets
are welded like her veins, all the blue charts of
summer.
Her hopes are high among fragments of skin, warts
and the mating of bone.
Cushions and overtures, the peeling of photographs
from a weathered hand. The shriek of a plant
in bud. A red eclipse. Blue moons, turning.
I have borrowed so many tissues, she confesses, the
garden leaning sideways, sapless, like an anaemic
child.
A radio-active plant, hoping for redemption.
The master of ceremonies lost among her white corpuscles
looking for the audience.
The dialogue of seeds exploding.
An advancing geranium that will not lie down, creaking
on metal roots.
Her brain carries the flag of truce.
In the beginning was a cell, an amoebic day. But it
demanded clothes, and toys, and finally copulation.

Friday

And the giant shrinks into her hand.
Spread like a specimen, open and fit to be used.
Her album has a space for him. He makes the sign
of the cross as he is glued to the page. And all
the small shining parts of him remind her of royal
days, frequent fountains, her skirt split, the road
to oblivion, hands like fire-crackers, blood clotting
like leaf-scars, staccato messages stained with
blood, a telephone at war, the sun hammering at her
ear, words divorced from their home-ground, the lap
of a wound, entrance by proxy, landscapes of figures

too thin to hold her, a theatre turned sideways, a
slice of scarlet petticoat and the leg it contained,
the heart's back door.
She will not forget the giant, pressed into service,
caught in her book like a frozen moth.

Saturday

The stars are turning. The galaxy that lives in
a block of quartz deep in the granite hill, is
changing its course.
Bags within bags. Boxes within stones. Bags
within crystals. A small bag that moves inside
the blue electric womb. Plants robbed of their
midnight expeditions. Bags stuffed with bunches
of thick air. A large granite tomb that is a bag
of bones and petrified dreams. A small bag made of
beads that lets the blood through. This wobbly
bag that is my head, trying for its future. The
punch-bag, the bag that is a beetle squeezed in a
child's hand. The bag that is the sun leaking,
full of holes, the marriage-bag for a new mixture,
the dream-bag that dribbles over breakfast, castrated
bags that are only one sex and contain silences. My
mother's bag that still grips my skin with itchy cloth
fingers. The bags that are full of cocks and have
no openings.
The stars are unravelling. This humming bag under
my skin blown to a ball, drum-tight, demands that
blood be spilt, that a name be let loose.
Demands the burst seed and an hourglass.

Sunday

Years humming in the bone-marrow.
An androgenous moon, bleeding.
The falling of thin electric rain on sundials,
on timetables, and trees that are busy writing
their new scripts under the earth.

34

BLADE

A babble of alabaster moons.
The pale shock thin as a scripture.
A night wound up, the snake-night rears.
Coiling of honeysuckle, a bracelet of
            budding words.

She is a knife, he said, to cut off my
            cankerous rose,
and took it, and plucked it
and laid it to rest in its coffin
            of milk and waxy laughter.

I am a thin sliver of bone, he said
and rattled his glass jar like a
            dying bead.
His huge bowl filled with an amber sea
and the sun set, his red silk heart
            like a flag.

From HOUSE OF TWELVE NAMES

She makes her house woven
from one thread. Her
twelve names can be sounded
this way and that, over
again, enduring.
He makes his house of
parts, once only. It
will not hold.
We need perhaps both
kinds of dwelling.

1. THORN HOUSE

And the house said, I am a cathedral of stars.
my windows are arched in love and pointed in exaltation.

I ask you to walk soft-shoed. I ask for your nun's heart.
these walls take inscription carefully. I have placed a
statue of wax-words close to the fire. they will melt
to the floor and be madness.

I am meeting acquaintances of the rock-age. splintery
men, whose heart is accurate. I meet a new steely
wind of the old rock. it brings the earth humming.
I pacify this irate stone guest. I will bring flowers
next year, and my cold slab will wear a flame to speak
with. I will lay it on your grave, you blue men, and
you will speak of gorse.
My words are shattered by the knife-flame.
the house folds and ignites, wearing a visor of thorns.

3. TOY HOUSE

This morning she discourages the sky.
remains of the child's toys, an embroidered elephant,
gallop across the lawn.
the face of the dark man sings last night's danger,
behind the sun.
she uncrosses her tangled stars.
the moon writes a belated warning, dying.

8. SPELL HOUSE

I give him my brandyglass. my sunbowl.
the sleuth within the ring.
a contamination of stars.
this day of spells elaborates.

10. MUSIC HOUSE

I am made like a dulcimer.
I chime your visitations.
master of separation, I crown you with a noble thorn.
you speak angular spaces into my books. you insinuate.
I find twelve stones from the seashore.
twelve flights of a quartz-woman.

12. ROSE HOUSE

Twelve roses haunt me. twelve bruises on the tree's
bark will denounce my intention. the tree splits,
tearing our rose-berries, born of a double-helix, a
twin-rose message creasing the air, the room penetrated
by dark futures. we make our way through the day
carefully, preserving hymns and peacock monstrosities
to read by. we are illuminated by a penumbra, a
violence of shadow.
you said goodbye like the interior of a candle. your
bite was a chip of the old altar. your roses blow
heiroglyphs into my torn face and the road that creeps
in from the east stops short at my living-room.
I am waiting in this matrix of silence for the wound to
remember. your name is a patchwork of instruction.
I can speak silences easily. I can make new beds under
the rib of the tree. I am a woman haunted by jasmine
and a crying skull. this day I am washed by tears, my
new face hums for its birth.

SHE TRIES

She tries it many times
flaps at her wings and oils the carpet with sweat.
It pours rivers through the boards
and still she is floorbound.

She is a crow. A plain bird.
Ninetynine blinks of a black wing
won't fly her. On the floor
are rusty chalkmarks; she needs
to get very close to read what
they say, they are so familiar.

They keep her caged upstairs;
the lining is torn on the livingroom
curtains, where she tried to get out.
She has raven's hair, and they say
she's too old to wear it loose like that.

Sometimes a song will ooze through
the pores of the house, and her
croak is of joy. Then she has
carved an arc to the ceiling, there
are a few feathers where the plaster cracks.

FOREWORD FOR THE PHANTOM CAPTAIN

Marianne called her fish Manda and it bit off her hand.
a nail grew from the spot like an iron flower. the
phantom captain was seen often in the garden wearing
his luminous overalls.
I must write this foreword with my back turned, she said,
disguising her pen as a conductor's baton or hiding it
between large slabs of marble paper.
I must write a multi-dimensional foreword, she said,
that he will recognise. a foreword like a tinkling
glass house, or the inside of a mirrorcage. and she
folded the paper until her foreword was a large black
dot in which were all the words the phantom captain
had ever written.

Some thought that pc stood for police constable and
attacked the phantom captain with words bound in iron
sheaths that rattled in his head like metal beads.
But Marianne saw that he was an invisible orator and
put IO firmly at the beginning of her foreword. then
when nothing else followed, hung the letters over the
door. they clanged in the wind like large bells.
then she hung them round her neck, and words dripped
out of them and trickled down inside her blouse and
settled in her belly like a small lake.
I must swim in this foreword, she said, and turned on
many radios at once. the words filled the room and
filled her head like a clutch of dictionaries.
and in the middle the phantom captain jumped in an
inky gavotte.

He entered the house on a wave of words and would not
be removed. he would appear between her thighs at
the moment of orgasm. he swam in the lavatory bowl.
he folded his thin faces between the paper leaves
and projected his sepia images on to the walls over
the gramophone. he rained forewords on her like
bullets, and carried a large white foreword from which

all the words had been erased, and it gave off a beam
into her head which sent all the newborn words
scurrying back into their hidden corners.

This month of April, she said, swims in my head like
a foreword.

She moved backwards through the book, licking the
pages clean. and when she reached the foreword she
stopped, settled into the page and posted a cardboard
cutout of herself to the phantom captain made out of
the words that got left behind in the rush.

NIGHTRIDE

He took the sky in his teeth;
he bit off a huge piece of it
and the journey was on.

In his rock prison, he crunched
the black slice of night
and spat out the stars.

He didn't notice that
the dark had filled him,
the walls were gone;

he thought it was only
sleep that lifted him,
cradled him through the dark,

where he flew, thought
the rocks and boulders on his way
were only shadows of themselves.

He spun on and up,
the dark inner night of himself
so dense, that at the heart

came one small star,
a minute flame,
his opposite,
a world he'd overlooked.

KINGS AND QUEENS
AND HOUSES OF PLEASURE

1

Curtsey to the gentleman, cried my red lady, wearing
nothing but the American flag.
But the film came out blue and sold a million copies.
and a million soft skirts flew in the wind for the
sake of the dream.

2

There is an island made of glass where the talking
mirrors are. There is an island made of lace
where the sun escapes. And there is an island
made of earth which is watered by one drop of
blood squeezed out of the dream.

3

There is only one, she said. And we take care
of it in turn. It is of ricepaper and bullrushes
and the moon that has lost its voice. There is
only one. And we take care of it between us with
our paper lips and fat kisses.

4

There is much merry-making between her legs. She
summons her sister who will speak for her. Unlock
the cabinet and let out the dream, she says. The
room floods from under her skirt and she lies like
a great tap with the washer missing. Her sister
sits on dry land over the mantlepiece, which escaped
and was secular. Only the voices
and the names are allowed drowning. And the vast
crowd of admirers who have never seen such a river
from any house of pleasure.

5

It rains often. It rains under the beds and
inside the cabinets and behind the fringe-curtains
and makes the blue water-women sigh in their sleep.
She sees fountains of dried flowers like a transmission.
Her head is full of mould and securities.

6

Here is a chequered room, waiting for worship. The
immense fortune waiting to be fed. She will dance
with a devil and exchange him for a prime minister.
The meal is made of fat cake and the national anthem.
She is a queen in leather and bonds, loyalty making
her skirts rattle like an orchestra of money.
She forgets his name and the notes settle like
flies over the black apples and the white oranges
and the black and white birthday cake flickering
in the middle of the hermaphrodite room.

7

A woman open to the night sky.
Her birthday is ready. He waits in the wings for
the first candle, carrying sunflowers. Morning
creeps over her skin looking for an introduction.
The king's yellow flowers bloom in the shadows
like words in the dream. She wakes and forgets.
Except that her room smells of sun.

8

She sharpened her heels and wore black to erase
him. The staircase smelt of leather and a threat
of water. Upstairs, she drew inky letters and
made tea and brooded in a dark corner. Her mouth
hung like a red poppy over the bed. He smelled
seeds and poison and long elastic hours putting
her pieces together.

9

God save the mirrors and all dark women, sang
the choir in the vicar's new church. He brushed
them hurriedly from his head like a swarm of white
butterflies.
God save entrances and holy water, sang the
madonna, shedding bloodred stones that hurt his
head. He hung a purple cloth over her for
abstinence and royalty.
God save all shadows and houses of pleasure, sang
a voice from the crucifix, and the vicar ran from
his church shedding his skirts and his prayers.

MAN OF ROOMS

It is a great joy, she said, to know that your
rooms are empty, and ripped the icicles from her
fingers like peeling a thin spikey glove.

I invited you, he said from the far end of a cool
clean corridor that smelt of pine forests and
contained many photographs of him among the
dripping needles.

His voice injected itself above her left ear. her
nose was bombarded by petals of mountainflowers.

You keep a clean polished clock, and know how
to time me in and out.
Your rosefingers are already infected by worm
dear, the time tells me so, he said.

Tell me of the room below, the dark lace room, she
said. where I can see a shadow-play among the
walls.

There I sing hymns to a yellowing ivory smile which
attaches itself to all my friends and makes the
piano quaver.

Do you wear it when I come picking, she asked.

It is my mask for writing you out. it is
tomorrow's face shaped and ready.

Really, she said, you might furnish the guest-room
better, and lay to sleep on a rattling bed of his
bones.

BLUEPRINT ONE

He makes a sound like transparent leather.
it is like MANY OF HIM laughing.
and there is laughter coming like an electric dawn
which stretches until my skull agrees to it.

A WORD IS A BLACK HOLE IN THE SPACE OF THE MIND

tears wash the face of masks.
I sell my red handkerchief in exchange for snow
which melts and is the earth's tears.
tears are unborn words expelled without ripening.
tears that do not fall creep over the eye-surface
and solidify and the world is seen through the
lava-beds of unmade suns.

MY NOTEBOOK BELLOWS FOR THE RED HANDKERCHIEF
THAT WILL NOT WEAR BLOOD AND THE SWORD THAT WILL
DEVOUR IT

I am shedding tears under the shelter of my head
and appear like a crab out of its shell
threatened by the sea.

He makes a sound like tired windows and the
picture-seller coming.

THAT MAN'S HEAD EQUALS MINE AND I WILL BARGAIN
FOR IT

the tears are a canopy under which the man and
his sister make love uninterrupted. I would
like to buy you a crystal moon he says, so that
you could wear it over your head like a vase
and your face would splinter and fragment and
say new words to me.

THE IMAGE-BANK IS DRY WITH UNSHED TEARS

I am wearing too many knives. they point from
my ears and my hair and are cutting down vegetation
wherever I pass until the edges of the roads are
wastelands of unshed words.

and he sheds tears of ink that make blots all over
her blouse and she can read there the times when
the words hid and would not come out, and the times
when the sun bleached his pages clean of them.

NUCLEUS

Heard among stones soft screams of juices running
Heard among skies the berry-lips torn
Heard among petals a miniature marriage
A woman parted born of the turning of sun

Seen among roots the skull muttering
Seen among seeds the gathering-in of rooms
Seen among skirts an embryo army
A gun set apart born of a turning of nails

Known among dolls the first choice
Known among books the murder of mice
Known among love the taste of bloods
Swallowing whole the blistered nursery and
            a dead star

Felt among blankets the new nerve of morning
Chosen among skins the throbbing neck-stone
Discovered among fingers a seventh pulse
Wanted among darkness, the whole explosion

VISITS OF AN ANTE-NATAL KIND

The doctor contaminates, using a tongue of snakey steel.
I ask for an illness that will not belong to me
completely. Just a borrowed inconvenience, a
short walk among honourable vampires.
Dear doctor, lend me a bubble of germs, that will
burst when I have recognised the visitors.
I bow to your stethoscopic words, your breath
humming with micro-creatures. You blow landscapes
over my cold bones. Your jacket smells of
chemistry and fever.
The doctor told me that in order to be ill I must
protect myself with fanatical care against all the
forces hammering at my skin. I must wear amulets
and talismans. I must make a door which will
carry a nest of locks, so that the keys weigh heavy
in my knitted bag.
I must gather pearly vitamins and keep them in glass
jars on the fortified table and worship them. I
must spray the ants that cling to the path and my
vest. I must sing songs that only the bees can
hear, and they will die and make no more honey to
sweeten me. On no account must the wind, which
is called draught when it grows very thin and mean,
be allowed to enter. And the faces of friends
must not enter, only turned sideways sliced into
paper that can reach inside through the letter-box.

And the streets are full of sun, smiling. Dangerous,
so the doctor said. And unexpected shadows that are
called people, who may well intersect your path.
They may try to sell you love-words, or poems, or
give you a piece of themselves. On no account let them
near, they will prevent contamination. Your best
defence is a barrage of instruction. At such times you
are justified in using the ultimate weapon. It will
do the job of a nuclear warhead – it will annihilate.
It is called fact, and you may rain pellets of it

on all uncovered heads that threaten you with barbs
of innocent greeting.
If you follow my instructions to the letter, you will
surely be diseased.
But only a small contagion, I ask, that I can put away
when I am tired of it. But the doctor did not hear.
You can even lock the walls of your head so that no
sound can enter. You will see birds leaning sideways
with no songs. And the tree will lash lame against
your eardrums, stiff with unhearing. And your snail-
window will grow a coat of green like a sick rose.
That seems to be going a bit far, I said.
Perhaps I don't need a doctor.
Perhaps I can find a milder version of this
disease under a frogstone, or the bright cesspools.

Only I can dispense disease, shouted the doctor,
polishing his prescription, holding his sterilised
pen ready to inject.
You must follow the instructions carefully, or you
will never be ill. Death is not guaranteed. And
his eyes spun behind his spectacles like twin nipples
of steel.

HOUSE OF EFFIGIES

He is kissed by the bite of the wild woman
And carries his loves to bed.
There is a sound like air falling.
Her hollows are a gathering of fish,
Her bright island incinerates.

He receives her wounds like a supplicant.
She bites out his dream
And spits it to the wind.
She makes him a cover of muskroses.

Swans across the water.
A ring of curled buds.
The child dances in a mesh of suns.
The camelia watches from its waxy heart.

SONG OF A FORGOTTEN LOVER

She waits at the door of his brown satin coat.
he will dance me to earth, she tells the brown fountain
full of dead seahorses.
I could see he would not reach the end of me. the
flame snuffed at her feet. the grass grew coral
ruffs.
I am dressed for his absence, she, sticking her
face to the glass.
a dying night ornament tells him her skin is mauve.
creatures pirouetting beneath the surface. his face
opened, trumpeted like a large pink convulvulus.
his voice grew sleepy as a cabbage rose.

he would live in the corner, and solidify. his
pitted heels itch.
he would freeze his hands into wooden sticks and
tap out messages to her. she is carved into his
boney chair.

I am orchard woman.
you were a water man, running.
I like the dry husk days. the wrinkled conversations.
love knots.
you wound my wirey walks with sea incisions.
salt stings will kill my orchard.
she sneezes, and an apple splits throwing small
bone pips into his eye.

he would keep one of her skins in the library folded
between the pages of the encyclopaedia. thin tissue
for reference. he would keep her eyes as paper
weights. all his quiet hours would sing through
their blue spiral. she would give him back his words
polished and crystalline. his mineral oratory.

I am woman blistered by hot salt. out of the orifice
of his ebony doll. streaming black words hanging like

rag-talismans. he talking to the white frill of her
new mended heart.
she sits in his leather pouch crying smokerings.
she hums among the shreds of his beard.
he will fill her lungs with sand deposits. she
will sink to the bottom of his cup. she will
wear creaking roses as he creeps to bed.

I am woman raped by a sand castle maker. torn by
a blue sea bird. pecked by the gritty hymns you
use to stroke me. I am eaten by your hungry
underskirts, your tartan vest. diluted by your
misty convolutions. the descent. heavy prints
sewn into my underskin, the blue-print world.
you sucked me out by the mouth and crunched the
shell for your evening communion. I hurt in my
separate palaces, ready.

he will wear her for his birth carnival.
she will stream down his ducts and be salt finally.
she will be spat into the night like a black velvet
curse. he will rub her skins until they reflect
him. and make her swell until she fills his
cupboards with black breath.
the bead rolls and tumbles down his face leaving
a scar like an old brown snake.
her eyes cover the library desk with stones. he
clicks them together, transmitting his messages
into her reflection, preserved in the brown wooden
table.

THE KING RISES

1
His face is dark and lined with small rooms.
And they shine through me like glass
Like the amber blood of moons. Like
The slow wink of a quartz.
It sings high and reedy in its vase
This quartz-flower. They are a flight
Of birds waiting there.
And the salt is a flower, a budding rock.
It has eaten the grass and the bed and the moon.
This salt altar will take us there.
This song will hide your nails.

2
It is a dark day full of the wings of birds.
They are like the books' leaves that cover the sky.
He closes the covers and waits for the lights to go out.
This is his altar day, where he rises.
The sun his shadow, the exquisite corpse.
He worships with gorse candles, they tickle his skin;
So his hymn laughs to the hills
And comes back a brewing storm, and settles.
And I am the priestess of his beard
And must wait outside his window.
The skirt of his game, his protective cloth.

3
He makes night music of the scare crow,
Night music of the mad bird, cry of birdrags,
Where they tatter his windows up, and creak
Through his laces, his peacock shirts.
He wears them now, of cream and silk.
He wears them to bed, and they lace him round
With speeches, and stiff swallows of slippery food,
He eats her eggs, wearing his plaster shirt.
And his neck is stiff with her face inside it.

He clamps his own to the collar, red as a paper,
But she shines through whitely, a rose
That blooms luminous and many-tongued.
This is his hidden mouth, and he takes it out in the morning,
It doesn't speak, only kisses her eggs
That will break gently into his dark bowl.
And all this dreaming at his glass,
Holding his oracle liquor, the noisy wine
That scrapes his hours; a red music.

4
This stone polishes him.
It wipes him gently amber from the fingers up.
This stone is a powerful blade to set
The king free. His vine ropes hold the house
And his knotty hands. There are bands
Of silver sweat dripping his face away.
His wax face weeps amber tears. I collect
The stones for a necklace that will talk of him.
His words take my neck in their hands.

5
The king is in his counting house.
He collects my breath as he passes
And stores it in bottles. It is
His charm for the use of me.
So I whisper him dark when he blows me
Over the flowers, and they stir
With my many voices.
The king listens. He uses an old coinage
And I am part of its glint.
His head buzzes with all the flies
He disturbed with my bright falling.
And all the garden things wear a cover
Of golden rust.

6
The king aches.
He appoints musicians.

He appoints skies and mountains
And books to disguise them.
And sets an arrow in her skirts,
Winds up the bridal bed
And they fall there the petals
In the hour-glass of his head.
This night of nails and promises
Was made for him. He has travelled
The game through, and undone all the buds.
He has wept his twin stars to bed.

So he lies among his stars at last
Dreaming of who he came from.

A MONTH OF SMALL GUESTS

She is walking her bride-beast to the edge.
She is taking words out of sockets in her wall
            and planting them in her carpet.
There is a huge burst of sunfire from the gilt mirror
and the plaster ducks are seen over the west
            in strict formation.

I am out of bounds, she says
and draws in the nets full of crisp dresses
and the canopy of stitched eyes.
She takes a cupful of dark patterns, noisy wine,
a pulpy finger and a book of gardens.
The stairs lead to an urn, the passage is an
            infinite cradle of daggers.
This, she says, makes my skin itch, and burst
            into chattering flames.
This, she says, is my oily ointment, made
            for the dark.
And sits in her star, and wishes the papers,
            and blows the tissues into roses.

AXIS

I am faint as a fly on the sky's retina
a blue child hatched in paralysis
I am small as a room without windows
as a widow's wish

An abdication of wings
The funereal candle pants
It is the remembering
of all flame, slowly

One after the other
each flower sucked colourless
A pale woman stares
at her bleached gloves

In the dark bowl
lips endlessly receiving
a landscape shrunk
to one microscopic word

The soft hammer of a moth
It is summer, inhaling
It is the annunciation
of a birth, slowly

RED WHORE IN A HIGH MONTH

I have red boots
they shine in the blackness like dark blood
I have a red smile that burns the shadows
I have a red nail that blisters

I married him, flimsy as a blown flower
a brown staircase leading to a brown room
yes I have let his brown fingers enter
and his brown back carry me
yes I am brown. like a madonna

Do me the favour
make the morning glass
give me back my skins
the crucifixion does not take place
this time, only the dice
and the robe
this flame does not consume
this time, only the shrinking moon

The room full of leaves
of ribs
I am carved into the chair
I am waiting for my blood to arrive
I am screaming
the size of laughter

The clock spits
eaten by worm dear
he is planting a small bush
in the castellation of stone

I thought the sunflower
had eaten you, he said
painting the petals red
crawling into my head

THE WEDDING

I sing my song through a molten copper ring,
she said. She took the beetle and polished
her chains.

I will approach this woman, he said, and stroked
the air. He rubbed the brass lamp and made the
dark rear up. He threw his brocade shirts
ahead of him.

I must speak to her, he said, and sang out a
song of many colours, made a knot in the space
between them and cut a splinter from its dark
heart.

She polished her wedding dress and waxed the
flowers. She put a bell-jar over her face and
looked out pale as a cameo. It seems to be
getting darker, she said, and set a stone in her
eye.

I must behave, he said, as though there were an
hour-glass in my head. And hung from the
mantlepiece by a silken cord. Her face shone
like an alabaster clock over his head. He
wondered why there was such a scent of flower-
gardens. In the bell-jar she rang out her
secrets, turning the days into rosewood caskets.

ANCIENT VOICES OF THE CHILDREN

The mouth is crying
like a sack of bones
In the rivers of autumn
the mouth weeps for it

Leaves scuttle and worry
on the edge of history
like crabs or a sea-shock
Through them, the rib

Children a naked memory
for the floral skirts
For ice in august
this pristine hymn

Ancient voices of the
children, rubbing their
soft curse against the ear
catching the new-made tear

THE BRIDE MONTH

He made her an altar of two small lights. it was
5.30 in the morning. there was a dark blue laquer
box, of the night sky, and a small round box of
prayer. they hummed in the altar-mirror.
'I cannot speak' she said, and her words caught in
the altar light and shimmered.
And then there was a grey filigree web. she has
the curtains closed all day to keep it out. and
the forest key.
the stranger wears moss under her window like a
green disguise.

The bride waits. she waits with an accurate look
on her face. she will scatter scarlet petals over
her white silk sheets. the bride will introduce
a dark thread into her veil, dripping like creamy
lead. already they are caught in her trailing
cream armoury. she stands like a black geranium,
full of the soil.

And it was like crushing a pale flower in his fist,
mercilessly. her white blouse crumpled into a hot
white ball. the maroon buttons bleeding through
his fingers. and she had filtered through, a lily
in flight.
she sweeps out the yard and lays her mat in the square
of sun. she arranges her pillow and her cup of
songs. the altar unfolds from the tips of her hands
like a japanese water flower.

My small blue seed will hum in its box of ice, she
says. this month of many suns bursting.

APE-HARVEST

I cast my net and pull in an octopus with
            a name called black
he will not make blood of my claw-foot
nor cast me in ink
he will not call sea with his dark lip
nor wet my bone-button knee
I am dry as a word heron-boned

I uncurl foxy fingers
sly as a stone on an anthracite shore
I point to stars hot with rape
an unrepentant moon traces my ape-blood

I cast steel-nets and pull in the
            tide's rib
with a name called judge
pickings of torn sea-cat
the waves made flesh
an eye in the bone sea-palaces

Jaws tight as a pincer
face traced in a web of twine
and a name called skull

She grins like a small blue monkey
            under the catch

It is still now. of dust. the hills are weeping red
streamers. we have gleaned what we will from the falling
of fruit, the ears of corn. over-ripe bud scatters red rags
to the four ends where my fingers stroke the edge of you.
our bed bursts into seas.

I give you a flower. a red passion. I tremble a flame of
flowers on the burning edge. and dance for the heat. but
it is still between our separate places. scattered poppies
among the sun are wordtouches for the time. you look
transparent through them. sun flickers and flecks their
red. I give you a flower.

Dark it is. dark. stillbrooding. shadows creep out of
hollows gobble the grass and the waving sticks. they are
brittle and break. they burn easily. we are uneasy behind
curtains. flash of our hidden lightning opens the room.
snaps it shut. it is a howling of things brewing in darkness
and I am not ready. they creep round. I hide in velvet.
gabble and spew in a thunder of wounds. the tissue hurts.
the whine whirrs home. the candle is out. and the sting.

later you take me up. soft rags and tissue paper. a little
crackle of pain. infinite quiet. your hands are velvet
petals in infinite quiet.

Dust is heavy.
it is a thin carpet of needles on my toes
they rise through it scents of flowers

we are thirsty
the carpet weaves into fields
the poppies are sown

dark seeds are eaten and
our goblets drain the sun.

64

they fight over us still we are crumbled and raked through
gravel and leaves
she hangs from a livid sky is all dangling breasts and heavy
cloudlove he is quicksilver darts underarm and shivers our
back his is a thin shaft of steel needling underneath
between them we are hidden under paper leaves that turned
over yellow hearts and red flowers red and yellow the sun
is all green to us the white and the black witch conjured us
out of fireflies and flames

dark rainbows shine inside light arc curves over million
diamond icepeaks sliver of glass mirrors own reflection
inside out essence of yesterday's dreams wrapped in sticky
pictures floats on moonbeams
we dream of children and outtosea mockinggulls lull
honied dreams to ashes
outofthe dust the black innocence of burnedout days
ferments and steams spews a great compost heap of
outworn nerves an old lady sits in the mind's eye watching
with paleblue eyes out of my window tomorrow's shock my
old lady to come and clothe me asking only to dream of
seagulls her life a song of little blue roses sharp crystals of
young flights in the first wet grasses old woman found
dead in her home this morning

He and She Talk

He: Snap snap snap snap she is always coming undone

She: How you rode the tides always forward to the shore
      Not afraid of the sea

He: She tasted brittle of salty sand
      I was glad when the timbered journey ended
      She tasted of rust

She: Dusty skin and hot salt
      I was drowned in a large dark sea with no light
      Just dark waters endless over a vast expanse of dark . . .

He: Out I was out she bit hard and laid bare fangs
      Mother came down and prevented it
      Whisked out her pride and surrendered

Clipped on her mask like a snap-fastener
Cowered and whined, I slapped, she

She: Oh what a harsh crashing tearing of pain on
My face on my ideal of surrender
An interruption of utterly alien flesh
To the soft sinking moment before you hurt
I am hurt you should not we must we might if you
Don't I will couldn't you not have done that?

He: Like a bird a carrion stop the noise
Married for silence went to sea
Flowers of unborn love growing in the timbers
Distant woman shrieks on the shore
Woman looking woman wanting
Woman with great empty dark belly
Eating and hunting wanting devouring
Munch munch
I fear for my bones

She: Nice husband good to me
Love on Sundays
Wonder what he's
Doing now? Out there always
I can't settle
Try to find him
Watch the clock tick
Long time coming

He: She is a tight taut twining stem that creeps and curls
Round my body and squeezes The drag of time
Breathing heavy and do my duty
Out to the bellyaching sea
Spare the rest of my small water
My floating soul is small and murderblack

She: Found on Sunday husband did it hard done by

He: She did nothing

She: So ungrateful why'd he do it?
Such a passion
On a Sunday

He: She had the head of a snake at the end

She: Such a passion flowers and sand-dunes

He: Little suckers on her fingers
Clinging of vines of parasites

She: Spread sand pale as dust

He: She crumbled and cracked in the mirror of the sea

She: I thought I won him easily
Sure as summer pale yellow sun

He: As we went down dark her eyes flashed
Face cracked and split
Talons to the last

She: Stretched into the grave my water
Shadow on the glass

He: Dark bird over the water
Hovering and brooding

She: Suicide is such a disgrace to the family
They didn't know he did it

He: And she bobs and floats on the water
Where she was lost
Bobs in my head like a nodding boat on the tide

INTRUDER

The rasping of rusty choirs under the tide
Deep in the mirror a split unforgiven
Rooms within splinters frozen mid-flight
Words goose-stepping over her straw hair

A large slab of damp paper
Words like frogs in heat
a mud-melody
The envelope closes round
like a silk clamp

It is a hungry guest snapping skeleton jaws
It is thin and inches into her skin like a new knife

The letter is a wheel telling futures
Words fall like inky confetti

The cut flares like a rose

VOICES FROM THE COSMETIC GARDEN

Two butterflies collide in flightline. ragwing.
ripped silk. a mating of torn dances. garden
of shredded lightning.

woman sitting with print of worn poppies on her
left shoulder. flowers ride her skirt like a
summer tournament.

the grass complains. she asks for a bed of large
mouths to be planted where she can hear it. the
croquet lawn hisses for lost games. bees drip
gold velvet collars. her skirt is a journey of
stings.

the queen corn rises. dark of the earth sends
small purple flames to greet the guests.
she makes snake music. her tongue demands that
the sap be taken slowly.

woman dripping with ash–petals. woman eaten by
wounds of the hunting poppy. woman made mossy by
the green tree cloth.

they rattle their croquet bones.

man weeding his papers. his writing desk is
frosted with husks. nettles sit astride the
pens and inject his words with a poisonous bite.
the books pollinate.

she smiles like a crab apple.
her elaborate leaf confection quivers with every
breath of the sun.
the visitors number themselves by their bones and
stand on prepared afternoon pedestals.

she counts the way in and adds a crayon mark to his
left cheek. his blood lies at her feet red as a
jelly. her tongue will take him on to itself, a
tiny pearl of heat.

the man touches his violet shadow and cracks open
the fountain. water rips over his skin sewing the
torn ends. binding the scar. painting a silver
trail to make of him a luminous cacoon.

the trail of the mallet. she will wait with her
skirt a cool umbrella.

this man is a jigsaw. his middle road leads
like a black ribbon into crimson forests.
his unfinished days clatter, hang loose like
scraps of tinfoil in a wind. the sun bites into
his fading landscape. she comes with a brush to
touch up his pale corners. his angular pastel
bones, his diluted facade.
the woman wears black to make him an ebony doll.
her words swim in the moist glass tabletop like
charred maps.
she wears an ebony ring and will marry the day
priest, man of white cloth and a white bone whip,
man of a pearl-bound book with the story of his
early equestrian darks.

a copper garden, waiting to be burnt. waiting
for resurrection.

she is writing the plant names on to her skin.
they consume sap in thin glasses. their voices
scrape the bark.
I will win the garden for a looking-glass, she
says.

his monacle is a flying saucer bird. his buttons
add up to twelve and faithfully serve him. he
scratches her name on to the knob of his silver
cane. he gives each ant a reprieve. a thin film
of red lies over his mouth. he wears his skin
bone tight and the words squeeze through cracking
like shots.
this man is already enbalmed, she tells her pencil.
and it slides gently over him, making a crease
in the wax.

she peels off the garden like a mask. her face in
the mirror stares whitely out of the dark.

WINTER CANDLE

The candle wears red
for marriage
for keys
and the garments of opening

The candle is purple
for bad books
for apology
and the kiss of the left hand

The candle wears flame
for a shot
a white bullet
the tunnel of a fire-word

The candle wears red
for mourning
for undiscovered deaths

STONES ON MONDAY

We are seven
stonegates waiting through time
recording the heartbeat of the shore

1

Maps of my ancestral home
I face you, faceless
the palest of skin and rusty heiroglyphs

2

I am kissed by a tree
a thumb print
the blue lace rides my birdback
I carry the word with me from the sea

3

Red is of iron, of claws
red, for interior, brown sea-blood
I was wet when you picked me, red as a flare
now I put forth small glittering surfaces
to the sun

4

I am the one without a name
turn, turn again
a tomb, a riddle
a dusky ornament to all
the sea-clocks

5

Curled and crushed
pebble of many blows
drawn and cut
marked by a million tides
the smallest, carrying
one grain of fire from the sun

6

Once I was white
a limb of the white cliff
someone drew a red curtain
over my white skin
someone trod me with
a rusty heel

7

I am a tablet of the writer of sea-memories
the horizon of fish
I am spattered all over with attempts to explain
I move so slowly
trying to fathom the signs
I lie so heavily
I cannot remember my name

I AM HERE

Through the curtains of sun dust I see you
patterns of warfare. I spray the ants and
iron linen in this cramped afternoon to make
sure that I will be ready and clean of spells.
I stare at the stars and practice the
exercises of remembrance. I try to
remember black between stones, the name
whispered hot as a spy, the after-image
of your flesh-print under my heart.
I put a frame around my transparent hours
to know them better.

THE LADY CHOOSES HER STARS IN
MIDWINTER

> *Lend an ear to the land*
> *the berries are full of poverty*
> *the avenue full of fools dancing*
> *We live under a rapacious moon*
> *translator of candles*

1

I contain under my skull the dream of a friend.
Earth enters blood, thick as the sigh of the
ending season. All writing is unfolded, the
forest is betrothed. Blood enters earth and
shapes the heart of summer. The writing of
birds is seen as just another crime under the
cruel stars.

2

Unravelling the last wish sticking to the rim
of the bowl I discover I do not know her.
Neither the dream or the flesh. Neither his
smile or his eye.
For he was milked on magic and his touch is
a fermentation.
For his language is dry and his tongue is
a stone.
For his methods are under the shadow of things
where ants propagate.
And his shirt sticks to him like appleskin.
His name is thick as crust.

3

The massive gate with two lions that hammers
out the years. She grazes her knee on an iron
paw. Gravelly is the winter, grit on her skin.
The air fierce as a pumice stone.
Formally making the grass grow is hard work.

Harder than winning at dice. Harder than
pretending to weave daisies. Harder then
presentiment and naming flowers. Harder than
dropping the words one by one into the waiting
ear that carries them right to the heart,
where they take on their new colour.
The gate is of midwinter, locking the frost
in. The gate is a grandmother of iron,
guardian of tomorrow's game. The gate will
not remember such an infrequent visitor.

4
One leaf, left behind.
Obelisk and tissue, ghost and ambassador.
My nightdress streams under the white interpreter.
Words stretching and moaning over the torn field.
The leaf, the shell,
listening to devils, to dry dreams,
pausing only to announce
midwinter.
From here we move downhill into the graven image,
blue as a child. And here we begin weaving the
limbs of the betrothed. Listening to the far-off
candletalk. Hearing the dark beating. And the
leaf, the flickering pulse, a shiver on the skin
of the dark.
My shoes are white and need changing.
My gloves are showing the bones.
We begin weaving the cloths and the skirts,
the veil and the ice.
Forests groan with waiting.
Like priests their time grows into a massive
clock with no memory.
We begin weaving the new story.
The pulse stops. Winter is out.

THE DAY THAT LET SNOW FALL

In among the cold flowers
laid to rest under a sky of stone
a small heart that picks its way
among ashes, that collects talismans
that pins hyacinths to the women's
dresses, in memoriam

She explores the new limb
the breadwinner of dreams
the northern tip of the house
the locksmith

Alone on the iced hill
her thought throws steam
into the enemy air
and traces a path home
among the chips of ice

The room splinters and moans
Between the pieces of mirror
the parting of hair
the man's face flickers
The future comes and goes
comes and goes
giving a wreath and a bud
under one wing

She tries to trace his features
into the unwritten skin
She tries to conceive the phantom
The sky bears down
full of unready stars
Her body assembles
ready for conception

SHADOW OF THE WINTER BIRD

How many times have I travelled to the raven
the arch-house full of enemy weaponry
no yearly nesting among walls black as the hill

The glass-house and the raven
my compatriots
bearing soft messages above the crowd
until summer's end

I had thought of roses, rains
but it was too soft
it was the dark bird
the necessary visitor
handing me stones
crystal pictures
stems of intersection
ruled by the bird-eye
the winter mirror

I had wanted spring too soon
and there was still one more journey
I had still to name the letters flowing
free as the snow from my eyes

MEDITATION

I go out on to the hill taking my shadow.
the sun hammers. the sky and hill are
unfolded full-blown. there is silence
like a shell. something solidifies. a
small pearl forms in the base of my throat.
the grass rises to greet me. the hill is
a spiral I will meet it again. smaller
and smaller, I claim horizons as my
own.

THE GIRL WITHIN THE WHEEL

I am a circle
I am round as a night and a day
I am fresh as a ring
I am mud and apple-promises

I SIT ON THE HILL
RED INK, FOR MARRIAGES
I NUMBER THE STEPS DOWNWARD
INTO MY SHADOW
I NUMBER THE DAYS LEFT
FOR ME TO SIGH AND BREATHE NAMES
I WATCH BOTH MEN CRAWLING
BENEATH THE LEAVES

There is only one moon
the girl within the wheel
kisses slight as moths
promises thin as an axe
there is only one room
and no visitors

FLAMEFACE

I remember
candles in both our hearts

I remember
candles burning in our separate
windows

I remember
one candle
pulling the space
between us
into a ring

I remember walking
into the flame
it seared my finger
I cannot erase the name

QUEEN OF CLAY
for Peter Redgrove

And my room is red and warm she said
round and warm of the red earth
berries that fell and bled
the snake whose skin is shed
I wear a mask to capture your head
I am white acid she said, she said

The numbers fall tinkling into my lap
the stars ejaculate into my head
a land I outwitted bleeds through my flesh of silk
a house I deserted stretches an evening shadow into my lap
Twelve names, seven summers
the book writes me into itself, humming
I am the small girl, my own child-mother
I cradle my own heart under the sky
she runs into my lap, afraid of thunder
the roar of the heavens, the roar of blood falling
she feels my tears that fall for the earth that is dry
Question the blood and the winter
shall it be stone or a bright new ring
shall it weave corpses into the spring
shall I ride summers with whips or with stars?

And my room is round and blue she said
the blue of an ice-crystal
the shine of an ice-mirror
The child has gone to bed
the mother has turned her head
I am a white page she said, she said

SONG OF THE RAINMOTHER

Child among the bullrushes
child of the damp earth
child among the rains
my rain that I saw silvery like needles
yours that was black as chimneys

child among the stones
child of a granite love
child among crystals
learn to love whichever time of day you choose
learn to know your footprints early

child among pictures
child of postcards and paints
child among constellations
paint your portrait early where you want it
spit upon all the leaves that they may love you

She said, I learned my alphabet from my father, and drawing
lines around things. He was the master of boundaries,
the whip and the ring. I learned from my father to shoot
straight and put a price upon the heavens. Summer was best,
he said, it saved cloth. Summer was best because no
darkness to hide your young trembling lust, and the hands
that crept towards each other's were white birds caught in
the sun's glare. He kept an account of the skins I worked
through, my father's bull neck and twitching fingers. My
father's eyes that nosed among my skirts for blood. And
found small boys and footprints and a few broken twigs.
But he taught me to walk ten miles a day and that was useful.
And the ground that fell from under my feet opened chasms
I was later able to peer into. And I could love all my life
without getting tired. And his clear blue eyes shone,
pushing me forward. And the glass that tinkled on my
birthday was early music. And the room downstairs gave
many a lusty dream.

Cakes and candles. Fireplaces and a day of truce.
Lanterns were lit in the heart of the family. And smothered
by dark blood.
Lanterns were lit in the skirts of the women. And pigs
grunted under the moon.

We had two birds that died. Doves of remembrance.

We followed faithfully in all the right processions, under
the right flag. Carrying the right badges. My mother's
skin was pink then. Now it is written all over with all
her stories. Tiny letters that make shadows and lights
among the folds of her skin. She flickers softly like a
candle near a window open to the dark. She remembers
it was she who showed me the mud and the underclothes, my
room a barometer.

For you, father, rosettes and a white book, naked, unwritten.
For you, mother, ragwort and primroses, for you
                              never knew spring.

SUMMER OF GLASS AND A RING

She sings like a fruit
like a mid-morning sigh
She comes like a storm
like a meteor
Her opening is a flower
turned inside out
My journey ends
in a cavern of glass

SWING, AND THE PENDULUM CHILD

I creep near the roundabout,
it swings iron arms and swallows my child.
She runs races, she breathes. Her legs are thin.
she grows without my wish.
she speaks back at me, but the words
are stretched and tempered, cut and crystalline.
And the man pushes the roundabout faster,
an arrow in the sun.

I creep near the shadow that is the gift
of evening. I call a number, thinking of
cats'-cradles, the unwelcome invitation, the
days sparsely ordered with too much in
between.
Your candle splutters under my rib.

The house is quiet when I regain it,
orange-blossom spilling over the late meal.
A few addresses noted, a few stairs,
a few costumes, new colours, the flash
of iron bars across my eyes.
What did he say, that all conversation
is premature marriage? It is an endless
waiting-room, my words hooked on barbed-wire.
I recapture my child from the iron claws
only to dream that she died in an epidemic
in a cold blue room, after
I tried to give her amber honey
the life-blood of bees.

METAMORPHOSIS

Once was a woman who made me bricks,
a thin woman, a lithe woman, black as a spider.
She had patients and grew large that way.
She used to help people, and grew fat that way.
She became doctor, and died of love.

SCAVENGER-BIRDS

They drew near her, and the small glittering
stream that fell in the sun.
They wore thick skirts and boots, even though
the sun was hot and penetrating, enough to
tear through my child's dresses and turn her
hair to gold.
Sun, the penetrator.
But these girls were armoured as though they
might be touched too young. As though they
might feel fire and taste gooseberries, and
that would be divine intervention.
That would mean a world coloured blue and
gold like the old saints. She was never
arrayed like one of these, in her milky
flesh.
Her father knew the sun turned sour. Molten
sun like rust over the grass. Like a rash on
his child's face. His fist lashed out and
her small nose bled. She fell among all the
tumbling brick and stone, the hill swinging
sideways, feeling the father as a mountain
moving among the stars. Her face a crumpled
flower and the red wound.
He struck at the flame that mocked and
challenged his sun-tired skin, alien, replete.
He couldn't find the confessional and this
small globe burst, and spent itself.

KNOTS

There is something in the air which tells me I must
            not grin. Something
about the way the pavement smokes like an old indian.
a certain indefinable cathedral-dark, spreading in place of
            storms,
a crack in the chalk cliff, an uneasy telephone.
The way the light will not cling any more to my hair
as though the eye of the hill is slowly sinking shut
and the retreat of a million armies, leaving my skin.

There is something which tells me not to make spells today
not to encase the glandular dark hovering at the door,
a slight purple teasing my legs,
they are sticks and branches, I can see only trees.
The way the window seems like deep crystal
into which I can plunge my hand and pull out fish.
Better to stay quiet, and still, and see what it is, coming.

THE DREAM CHILDREN

The day of toads
the day of numbers
of arithmetic and eggs
of a boy drawn into the sea
of a man with painted lips
of music the perfect equation
of a house smaller than my head

The day when I loved by proxy
when I underestimated the power of the veil
The day when my teacher said that words speak through me
and how when I affirm my life I am castrated out of it
the day when my argument spread like a layer of thin jam
when I saw the face of my life in every candle
The day when I lay thin and stretched as a membrane over
          the picture of you

The day when I beat out my heart
held it and hammered it flat
took images eagerly from last year
The day I discovered a biography of you
in the sand, in the sky, in the white veils of women
Someone died in the sand, the day I recognised them
a little late, chasing each other among the flowers and stones.

HOURGLASS

The day I let out a pack of women with large mouths
The day I met my own shadow along a corridor that smelt
        of beeswax
The day my skin was stretched tight as a jungle drum
The day the space was too large and I saw myself in every
        blade of sun
The day I approached noon without accomplishment
The day the children vanished and left me staring into my
        heart
The day the parabola of silence caught me unawares
The day my flint-skin lay grey as an early pavement
The day I counted time on the fingers of one hand
The day I saw them walking, page after page, away from me

I trap a linguistic fly
between finger and thumb
a teacher of daylight

I catch at a dream
that flickers between
one day and the next

I see promises in the mahogany table, the day of sighs
I feel feet thunder under my rib where the breath stills
I hear armies on the horizons, the spring migration south
I am alone under the sun, watching the raven, my possessor

THE STORY THAT CAME FROM THE SEA

Rumour has it that the large iron brain stuffed
with books is about to undergo therapy.
The rods that have held that stuffing tight and
dense for thirty years are about to split into a
dream. god the father will put on the demon's
mask and dance around the maypole.
The son marries many times into himself.
You wait like a nervous hen for your straw words
to fall.

How factories will discharge themselves. China
dolls in their think-boxes show signs of epilepsy,
cracked joints, volcanic skin, eruptions.
Show signs of religion. Warts and absentism.
Rumour has it that all the great revolutionary
nations have cohered into one man and grandfather
and grandmother face each other across the
breakfast table carrying on the cold war.

Cold as a fish. Distant as five loaves.
The weight of air that is charged with fantasies
crushes to earth all those cracked ones holding
on to a splintering tree.
Rumour has it that all mushrooms have turned
bad. That the indian didn't walk up the side
of the mountain. That there is no such thing
as the edge. That the stars are our enemies and
black as the ultimate colour of graves.

In the dead of night your unshed dream dashes
itself against the skull trying to enter.
Rumour has it that your wife you carry with
you everywhere died of malnutrition.

Sharp as a tombstone,
is black as a doll.
a fascination for shoes for a thin woman,
a reptile-song from her box, large as innocence,
churning the mud into cream.

Ambrosia and divine unction; the game is offered,
scratching under the holy shirt sounds like hail from
heaven and the tree creaks and the bed unravels.
I wave to my thin sister disappearing down the sink.
all of it was my tide, my sculpture.
Only a very original unused shoe left, she said,
her gift, that stamped me black and blue and made
my crotch ache.

Now the air turns on itself. freezes into shapes,
silhouettes. the buried head among flowers, and I
am king.
curled into questions, I am king.
the underside of you, and I am king.
And I take my brother and my brother takes me;
the edge of the moon burning.
I remember my brother-snake.
hot summers where a child grew.
I remember the wedding that fell.
I remember my skin falling, inviting a red moon
to bed.

The priest murmurs under his raincoat. the
burning hill hisses like devils. shoes and
sanctity, lean and white as a blade. a
shadow hums all night under the pillow.
Black queen to roost below the stars.

THE TRANSFORMER

She filed the last collection under Z for the north star.
She memorised his name head-over-heels under the
          hammering sun.
Stones and cornflowers: hills unlocked from their dreams.
The glacial summer broods overhead.

Ice in my orange heart, ice on your brown face.
Blistering kisses. I understand salt.

It is an afternoon of apology and power. It is an
elaborate sun-message dispensed in the sovereign game.
I feel myself an army of pawns,
night-watcher, wedding-guest.
I feel the wound spread slow like silk,
hunter, hermaphrodite.

It was an invitation to watch corn-women,
scarecrows, black hunting birds;
an invitation to the white bed, the granite noon-day.

I felt confetti fall from my lip.
I shed the husk.
The cornfield tells me I am sister,
I am queen in disguise.
Now, on the next day's hill
she takes a new wife, forgetting.

Burning beneath my eyelid in the grain of the brown
wood table, flames into smokey air, into the streets and
holydays. My small queen she burned there, charred into the
tin-box, the soldier who deserted. The mask fitted like a
hand and her eyes were white-blind.
The flame cannot tell, cannot cope, cannot name. Cannot
build castles out of air or make flesh, can only point to the
hidden hooded corner, can only lick up the dust.

Be brave, he said out of his cowl, and I spelled autumn.
Be kind, he said out of his matchbox, and I witnessed an
execution. Be bloody, he said out of the opera-glass, and I
was suddenly able to rise from my clothes of ash.

And the flame lapped at the shore. Painted the book black.
Sneered at the ivory leaves, presented my footsteps along
the edge of the wood. Told of absent moths.

My arm is burning she said, pulling the chair nearer.
My face is burning she moaned, unhinging the moon.
My heart is burning she reported to the great space under
the wing of the fire, knowing no priests of mercy.

Burning within the cup, covering the clock-face, flames
into madrigals, into the limbs of daughters. The room
splits in two. There is heat and disorder. Hanging to the
chain that sees me through, counting neck-beads, the
flame presents me with my mask, the perfect alibi.

AN INVITATION TO TELL

I am more than an atomic sky, a noiseless particle
a faceless luminosity, a sheath of air
I have a tongue, I pronounce names
I fold my mother gently, paper-thin
into the bottom-drawer
I hold her frail as the moon

I can tell stories, invent my population
The autumn sky carries no ribbons
My child is no blonde innocent
she is capable of hatred, of eclipse

It is all here in the moment's stillness
the war that was a rumour
the entrenchment of faces into their moulds
floral pinafores and the stink of death
a shawl covered with flowers of hoar-frost
scarecrows at the edge of my heart

Dull and dry as a corpse, days of roses
Their faces stare at me like etchings in the wall
railings of light and shadow
music like needles on the leaves of plants

I am more than an equation, sum of memory
I have an unknown pulse to prove it
an anonymous place of pale yellow spring
And I can marry over again
my mother laid in a drawer paper-thin
Is there a name for the second birth?

SUNDAY OF GREY DREAMS

Will you buy me grey gloves
will you buy me smiles
will you buy me a fine white horse
          that breathes fire
will you create a candle in the gourd
melt the night frost
will you bear witness to the clean white berries of winter?

I was a day dream, a night parody
I watched the water make its new population
and the window unfolded its frost-flowers
I longed for the speech of friends who live like heroines
whose dresses are words, gossamer words
whose lips bend and twist scarlet under the air
whose native land spits them into my lap

Will you wait for me under the lamp
will you buy me nails
will you make me a fist of iron so that
          I may resist
will you construct a forest that will not burn
turn the pages slowly
will you see how the child turns, turns at candlemas?

A WEEK OF ROOMS

Monday

The room swam in a web of coaldust, charcoal and glass
snowflakes. The floor black as a night without moons.
Angels under dustsheets. Whenever I go down the stairs
that spiral under my heart like a snake, the wind rushes,
the dark wind that shreds me into families, species, galaxies.
The embryo wish. The furniture mahogany, heavy as my
benefactor's hand. I followed my caterpillar dream on
Monday.

Tuesday

Married and marionetted, she stitches all the sides of her
open bridal gown with the petals that fall like tears from the
room's broken heart. Tuesday leaves no room for laughter
and the broken mirror frowns like a grandfather, giving
her away.

Wednesday

The aunt who was made of liquorice and sherbert. The
room is a cradle of songs to wrap dolls in. One doll grew
lifesized, shiny with bruises. Wednesday's child lifts the
covers of night, and will not look the moon in the eye.
Too busy, she cried.
Playing at cradles today. Lace games and love knots.
Playing aunty.

Thursday

The room is a word in flight, a ragged bird of the stars.
The candle licks up the spiral staircases and defies the wind.
I could not spend an hour in that room without ascension.
The flight that is made of damp glass, of bees chattering, of
the cutlass and the knife of March.
Thursday shivers on the brink of adulthood, wanting
to remember.

Friday

She lies on the bed in the room of silver stars watching the
moon bleed through the window. She lies with the
window pane pressing cold against her chest. She lies with
the man who has disappeared, torn into matchbox silence.
She lies with the dark full of visitors who press against
the black to be let in, skulls crying, the shivering black
beast of winter, the cover not strong enough.
Friday's grave-child moans and makes her peace with
nightgowns.

Saturday

Flowers on the edge of a precipice.
The volcano makes a ring of singed petals.
The heart of the room, the flameface.
Do I belong to you? she asks the burning mirror.
The next day was to be judge, the silence.

Sunday

Dense as marble, space between words, the room vibrates
in its infinite haitus.
The walls breathe silence into their pores and Sunday
dreams. White as a collar, white as the lace border on the
bedcover, white as waiting, as a communion wish, white
as the pristine smile of her friend, white as mourning for
the light all torn, she turns to the knife. That is red. That
will open the closed white casket that is Sunday, ready.
Roses flame in the new fissure. A paralysis of
confrontation. Sunday is a severed head, and a mendicant
priest turned into stone.

HEARING THE WIND, THE BOOK CLOSES

And now I must close the book and let the red
and green letters have their way and let the
mad laboratory of my head sizzle in the sun.

And now I must close the book and let the death
of all the inside be the marriage dance.

I am made of this ink that dresses me in
black and proclaims sentence. I am made
of the thin transparency of these pages that
turn my life for me, folded under the black
names.

I am made of parchment.
my blood is yellow.
the gift turns on itself, whispering.

NICKI JACKOWSKA was born in Brighton in 1942.
She is the author of many pamphlets, broadsheets etc. Her work
has been frequently broadcast and she has won several prizes.
She also gives readings of her work. *The House That Manda Built*
is her first full-length collection. She lives in Brighton with her
husband and daughter.